Looking at Small Mammals

Marsupials

Sally Morgan

Chrysalis Education

Distributed in the United States by
Smart Apple Media
2140 Howard Drive West
North Mankato, Minnesota 56003

Text copyright © Sally Morgan 2004

Library of Congress Control Number: 2004040911

ISBN 1-59389-175-X

Editorial manager: Joyce Bentley
Series editor: Debbie Foy
Editors: Clare Lewis, Joseph Fullman
Designer: Wladek Szechter
Picture researcher: Sally Morgan
Illustrations: Woody

Picture acknowledgements:
Ecoscene: 14, 21B Edward Bent; 12 John Farmer; 27B
Michael Gore; 5T, 32 Simon Grove; 4 Alexandra Elliott
Jones; 3, 6, 9T, 11T, 13T, 16, 17T, 19B, 21T, 26, 27T
Wayne Lawler; 1, 5B, 7B, 9B, 15T Michael Maconachie;
7T Robert Pickett; 25T & B Kjell Sandved; 10, 17B, 18
Alan Towse. Front cover: B & TCL Wayne Lawler; TR
Robert Picket; TL, CL & CR Michael Maconachie;
TCR Alan Towse. Back cover: TCL Wayne Lawler; TR
Robert Pickett; TL Michael Maconachie; TCR Alan
Towse. Corbis: 13B Joe McDonald; 22 & 23B Martin
Harvey; 23T Eric and David Hosking. NHPA: 20 Bruce
Beehler. Still
Pictures: 2, 15B, 24 John Cancalosi; 19T Alain
Compost; 11B Gunter Ziesler.

Printed in China

Contents

Introducing marsupials   4

What are marsupials?   6

Where do marsupials live?   8

Plant eaters   10

Meat eaters   12

Seeing and smelling   14

Getting around   16

Living in trees   18

Coming out at night   20

Digging burrows   22

Baby marsupials   24

Big relatives   26

Investigate!   28

Marsupial facts   30

Glossary   31

Index   32

Introducing marsupials

Marsupials belong to a group of animals called **mammals.** Most mammals have four legs and are covered in hair. They give birth to live young.

Koalas spend most of their time in trees.

The wombat is a small, bearlike marsupial.

Young mammals feed on their mother's milk for the first months of their lives. There are many different types of marsupials. They vary in colour, size, and the food they eat. The koala and wombat are examples of marsupials.

The pademelon is a shy marsupial that lives in the rain forests of Australia. It comes out to feed at night.

5

What are marsupials?

All marsupials have a **pouch**. The pouch is a fold of skin, or pocket, in which they keep their young.

This wallaby has a youngster in its large pouch.

The kowari is a small marsupial with a squirrel-like head and a long tail. It lives in burrows.

The young feed on their mother's milk while they are safely hidden inside their mother's pouch. There are about 250 different types of marsupials. The smallest of all the marsupials is the tiny dasyure. The largest marsupial is the kangaroo.

The koala gives birth to one baby. It stays in her pouch for six months, and then it is carried on her back.

7

Where do marsupials live?

Marsupials are only found in certain parts of the world. Most marsupials live in Australia, but they are also found in New Zealand and parts of North and South America.

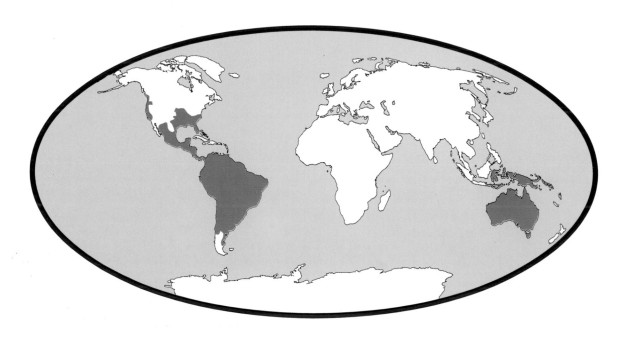

The areas shaded in pink on this map of the world show where marsupials live.

Agile wallabies live in Australia and New Guinea, where they are found in grasslands and forests.

Koalas are found in eucalyptus trees in Australia.

Marsupials live on land. They can be found in forests, mountains, grasslands, and in parks and backyards. Some can even survive in deserts.

Plant eaters

Some marsupials eat nothing but plants. They are called **herbivores**. The koala bear is a particularly fussy eater, since it only eats leaves from gum trees.

A koala carefully chooses a leaf, bites it off, and grinds it up with its teeth before swallowing it.

The bettong feeds on leaves, seeds, flowers, and roots.

Possums eat leaves, fruits, and bark. The honey possum is the size of a mouse and has a long tail. It also has a long tongue, which can reach down into flowers to sip the **nectar** and lick up pollen.

The honey possum comes out at night to feed on the pollen and nectar of flowers.

Meat eaters

Many marsupials are **carnivores.** This means they eat other animals. Carnivorous marsupials have sharp teeth to catch and hold their **prey**, and then to eat them!

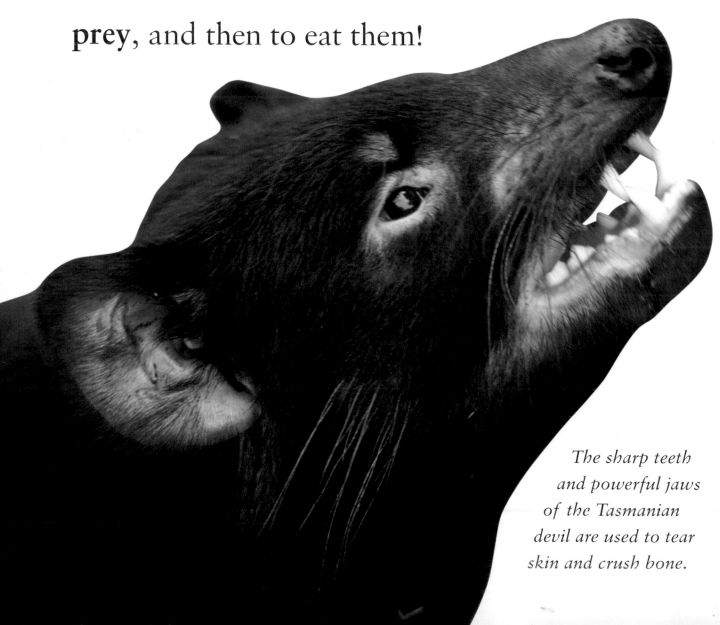

The sharp teeth and powerful jaws of the Tasmanian devil are used to tear skin and crush bone.

The antechinus, a type of dasyure, is an insect-eating marsupial.

They eat animals such as lizards, birds, small mammals, and insects. The largest carnivores include the Tasmanian devil and the quoll.

The Virginia opossum feeds on insects, mice, and rabbits. Sometimes it even kills chickens.

13

Seeing and smelling

Marsupials learn about their surroundings by using their senses. Many marsupials are **nocturnal**. This means that they hunt at night.

Sugar gliders leap from tree to tree. They have eyes that point forwards, to help them judge the distance between trees.

The koala has small, round eyes and a large, black nose.

Night hunters have large eyes to help them see in the dark. Many marsupials rely on their sense of smell to find their way and to locate food. The numbat uses smell to find its favorite food, termites. Bandicoots use smell to find spiders and worms in the soil.

The numbat uses its sense of smell and hearing to find termites, its favorite food.

Getting around

Marsupials move around in different ways.

Some hop and jump, and others waddle

slowly along the ground.

The agile wallaby hops along the ground using its long back legs and its tail for balance.

The rufous bettong spends its daytime in a nest and emerges at night to feed.

Some marsupials, such as wallabies and potoroos, have extra long back legs for jumping and hopping. Their long tail helps them to balance.

The wombat is a heavy animal with short, powerful legs. Although it runs slowly, it can travel long distances each night.

The wombat walks slowly with a waddle.

Living in trees

Many marsupials live in trees and are expert climbers. They have feet with long claws, so they can get a good grip on the tree trunk. A few marsupials have a tail that can grip branches.

Koalas climb by gripping the tree trunk with the claws of their front feet and bringing up their hind feet.

The tail is
just like a fifth leg.

The sugar glider can glide over distances of up to 50 yards (50 meters).

Sugar gliders glide
between trees. They have a flap of skin between their arms and legs that acts like a wing. This flap helps to keep the sugar glider in the air.

A brush-tailed possum uses its long tail to grip a piece of wood as it feeds.

Coming out at night

Nocturnal marsupials sleep during the day and come out at night to feed. It is safer to feed at night, because **predators** cannot see them.

This small, mouselike antechinus comes out at night to hunt insects, worms, and spiders.

The brush-tailed possum is a nighttime visitor to gardens and parks.

If they came out during the day, they could be spotted and eaten. Desert marsupials hide during the day to escape the heat of the sun. They come out at night because it is cooler.

The long-nosed bandicoot leaves cone-shaped holes in the ground while it hunts for insects at night.

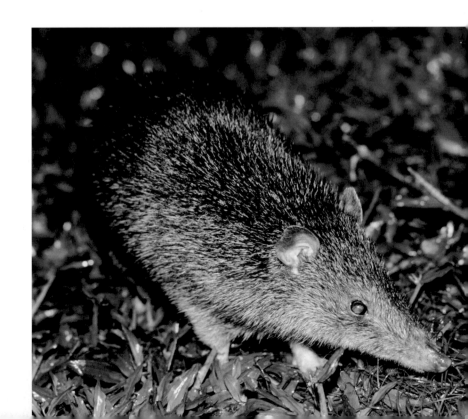

Digging burrows

Some marsupials dig **burrows** and tunnels in the ground. They use them to hide in, and to build their nests. The wombat has long claws, which it uses to dig through the soil.

The strong claws of the wombat are perfect for digging through soil.

The wombats' teeth are suited to chewing on tough grasses and roots.

They dig out a network of tunnels with lots of entrances. The marsupial mole has hands with extra-large, flat claws. It burrows through the soil to find food, but any tunnels the marsupial mole builds soon collapse.

The bilby builds a burrow that is about three yards (three meters) long and two yards (two meters) deep.

23

Baby marsupials

Marsupials give birth to tiny babies that crawl into their mother's pouch to feed on their mother's milk. They gradually get bigger until they fill the pouch.

A tiny brush-tailed possum sucks on its mothers teat to get milk when it is in the pouch.

Young Virginia opossums leave their mother's pouch when they are about 70 days old.

The babies may stay in the pouch for several months, until they are large enough to feed themselves.

When a young koala is six months old, it is carried around on its mother's back.

Big relatives

The largest marsupials are the kangaroos. The red kangaroo is 64 inches (160 centimeters) high and has a tail that is one yard (one meter) long. It can hop up to 55 miles per hour (88 kilometers per hour). Each leap can clear two cars.

The red kangaroo is the largest marsupial.

A kangaroo bounces across the ground using its long hind legs.

Kangaroos give birth to a single baby called a **joey**. The joey may spend six months in its mother's pouch.

A female Eastern gray kangaroo and her joey.

Investigate!

Living in the backyard

People who live in North America and Australia may be lucky enough to have marsupials living in their backyards. If you have marsupials in your backyard, you can watch them to see what they eat and how they move. In other parts of the world, marsupials can be seen in zoos and wildlife parks.

Watch how a marsupial moves around in a zoo, a wildlife park, or in your yard.

Pouches

You can pretend to have a pouch and see what it feels like to carry a young marsupial around. Tie a large apron around your waist, and place a stuffed toy in the pocket. Imagine what it would be like to be a marsupial with a pouch full of wriggling babies! How easy is it for you to move around?

See what it feels like to carry a baby around in a pouch.

Hops and leaps

Many marsupials have long back legs, and get around by hopping and leaping. See how far you can hop with your feet together. Can you hop farther if you hop on one leg?

Place your feet together and try bouncing like a kangaroo. How far can you leap with your feet together?

Find out about marsupials

You can learn more about marsupials by visiting a local library to read books on marsupials. You can also search for information on the Internet.

Marsupial facts

✓ The quokka was one of the first marsupials seen by Europeans when they arrived in Australia. They thought it was a rat.

✓ The musky rat-kangaroo is the only kangaroo that gives birth to twins.

✓ The yapok, or water opossum, swims and is the only marsupial with **webbed** feet.

These silhouettes show the size of a kangaroo and a Virginia opossum compared to a human.

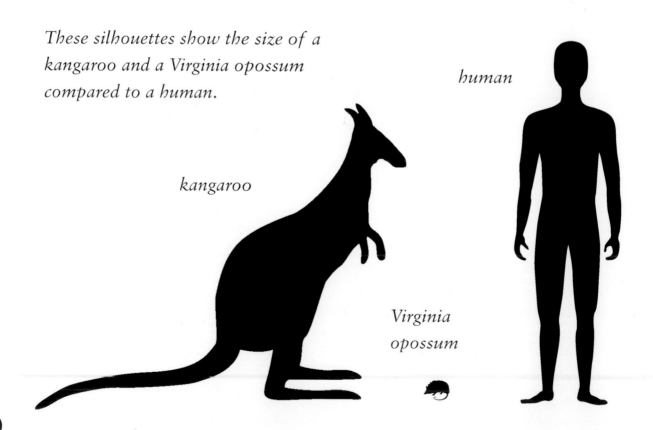

human

kangaroo

Virginia opossum

Glossary

burrow large hole or tunnel in the ground.

carnivore an animal that eats other animals.

herbivore an animal that only eats plants.

joey the name given to the young of a kangaroo.

mammal an animal that feeds their young with milk and is covered in fur.

marsupial a mammal that has a pouch.

nectar the sugary liquid produced by certain flowers.

nocturnal active at night, sleeps during the day.

pouch a small pocket or flap of skin on the stomach of a female marsupial.

predators animals that hunt and eat other animals for food.

prey an animal that is hunted by other animals.

webbed having flaps of skin between the toes.

Index

antechinus 13, 20

babies 6–7, 24–25, 27
bandicoots 15, 21
bettong 11, 17
birth 24
burrows 7, 22–23, 31

carnivores 12–13, 31
claws 18, 22
climbing 18–19

dasyure 7, 13

eyes 14, 15

food 10–13, 15
feet 30, 31

getting around 16–17
gliders 14, 19

herbivores 10–11, 31
hunting 14–15

joey 27, 31

jumping 16, 17, 26, 27, 29
kangaroos 7, 26–27, 30
koalas 4, 5, 7, 9, 10, 15, 18, 25
kowari 7

legs 16, 17

mammals 4–5, 31
marsupials 6–7, 21, 31
mole, marsupial 23

nocturnal animals 14–15, 20–21, 31
numbat 15

opossums 13, 25, 30

pademelon 5
possums 11, 19, 21, 24
potoroos 17
pouches 6–7, 24–25, 27, 29, 31

predators 20–21, 31
prey 12, 31

senses 14–15
size 7, 26, 30
smell 15
swimming 30

tails 16, 17, 18–19, 26
teeth 12

waddling 16, 17
wallabies 6, 9, 16, 17
wombats 5, 17, 22–23

yapok 30

zoos 28